My Many Boyfriends

My Many Boyfriends

The Punniest Book in Town

Anita Jacobs

VANTAGE PRESS
New York

This is a work of fiction. Any similarity between the characters appearing herein and any real persons, living or dead, is purely coincidental.

FIRST EDITION

Published by Vantage Press, Inc.
419 Park Ave. South, New York, NY 10016

Manufactured in the United States of America
ISBN: 0-533-15004-3

Library of Congress Catalog Card No.: 2004095590

0 9 8 7 6 5 4 3 2

To Alvin Jacobs, my favorite boyfriend of all

Acknowledgments

To my husband, Alvin, who had the pleasure or misfortune of being awakened many nights to hear my latest pun. Thanks, Al, for your encouragement, appreciative laughter, and for being my best audience.

To my daughter, Donna, for her consistent encouragement and support, her endless hours of editing and re-editing, and for showing sincere admiration for "her mother's" sense of humor and talent.

To John, my massage therapist, who gave me the idea to put my puns into the context of a story when I told him he rubbed me the wrong way.

To all of my friends who promised to buy a copy of this book when it was published.

My Many Boyfriends

I am not a young woman. I've been around the block a few times, and I must admit, I have always liked men. Many men, as the title of my book suggests. And I guess the attraction was mutual as I have had more than 200 boyfriends in my lifetime.

It all started at a very young age, probably in my teens. He was my SCHOOL TEACHER. I liked to be around him, so I would walk up real close, so that I could see his pupils. He was in a class by himself.

Then there was my FRENCH TEACHER. It was often really difficult to sit through his long class right before lunch, or so my bladder thought. When I asked him if I could go to the bathroom, he said, "Mais, wee, wee." I was a chatterbox and always talking in class, so my teacher made me write, "I will not talk in class" fifty times on the blackboard. Most people turn red when they are embarrassed, but I turned chalk white.

In my day, every desk in school had a built-in ink well. The INK SUPPLIER would routinely fill them and he really liked me, but he was nothing but a little squirt.

My family wasn't wealthy and I wanted my own spending money. So, after completing high school, I went to look for my first job. I was hired by a CLOCK MAKER.

The timing was right! It only took one second to know that I would like my boss. He paid me by the hour. We started dating, but he got ticked off, with me, because I tocked too much.

The real reason I was asked to leave that job was that I was called up for jury duty and I couldn't get the time off work, even though I begged the judge. But maybe it all worked out for a reason, because the JUDGE and I looked at each other and there was instant attraction. So that there was no conflict of interest we waited until after I served on the jury before dating. We went out several times, but he talked so much, I couldn't get a sentence in. He was odd, he liked to disrobe in front of me, and that's the truth, the whole truth and nothing but the truth, so help me God.

Through him, I met some really nice LAWYERS. One of them dated me quite a lot but then he stopped courting me. After not seeing him for a few weeks, he pleaded with me to take him back, but I was already taken with one of his young, new colleagues. This guy, however, was a heavy drinker, so I was really surprised when I heard he passed the bar. My boyfriend the LAWYER, he would never order one beer. He would always order a case.

Then I went to see my NOTARY. He was a fast worker. After only a few months, he asked me to marry him. I said:

"In deed, I will!" Obviously, nothing ever came of that romance. The BAILIFF was complaining about what sounded like neurological symptoms. I was worried that he might have a seizure.

Once jury duty was over, I had to find another job. I

eventually got hired by a CALLIGRAPHER who needed help organizing all his different inks. He was also nothing but a little squirt. I liked the job and began to make some money, so I thought about opening a savings account.

I went to my neighborhood branch and was introduced to the BANK MANAGER. He explained to me about savings and investments and then the inevitable happened. We were attracted to one another. We went on a couple of dates, but when he told me he had a wife, I told him to leave me a loan or I would teller. By that time anyway, I had lost interest in him. You can bank on that.

I was beginning to feel out of sorts, so I thought I should go to my GENERAL PRACTITIONER for a check up. After my experience with the courtroom, I realized I was feeling great fatigue and exhaustion. During my appointment, I knew there was something more than a professional relationship, and he told me that he was very interested in me and we started to see each other. I nagged him a lot, and after a few months, he lost patients with me. Quite frankly, he made me sick. But he knew my fatigue was still a problem, so he suggested that I see a HEMATOLOGIST. Breaking up with him was a bloody mess, but he wasn't my type anyway.

Then my skin started to feel dry and wrinkly, so I went to a DERMATOLOGIST. I was itching to go steady with him, but he said my behavior was rash. Besides my behavior, he said I was too skin-ny. After feeling around a little, he discovered a few lumps.

Although we were finished dating, he referred me to a SURGEON, as something didn't seem quite right. This doctor I really liked. His hands were all over me. He said he was feeling around for something. But when he cut off our relationship, I told him that was no way to operate.

To be safe, I was referred to a CARDIOLOGIST. Although I liked him and didn't have the heart to break up with him I told him to beat it.

My niece was not feeling well, so I offered to take her to her PEDIATRICIAN. Do I have to tell you the rest? Well, I will anyway. After dating him for a while, he told me he preferred younger women. I cried like a baby hearing that and came crawling back to him, but it didn't seem to change his mind. At first I thought he was only kidding, but that was the end of that affair. I guess he was just young at heart. There's just no pleasing some men.

After seeing and dating all those doctors, I thought I should go for a dental checkup. The first DENTIST I saw became my boyfriend. He wasn't a happy sort. He was always down in the mouth, but he did offer to fix my teeth for a buck. After having dinner one night, I asked him if he would like dessert. He said, "No thank you, the meal was very filling." He wasn't an easy mark. Getting a commitment out of him was like pulling teeth. And he was also very naïve. He believed in the tooth fairy.

Obviously things weren't going great for me so I decided to do some redecorating in my apartment. I thought it would improve my mood. I started by getting some new curtains for my windows, but the CURTAIN MAKER didn't hang around very long. The RUG MANUFACTURER was even worse. Naughty man, all he wanted to do was get laid.

Next came my UPHOLSTERER. He wasn't very well when we started dating, but then he fully recovered. I wasn't very sure if I liked him very much. It was his character. He was very materialistic and quite a fabricator.

I had limited closet space so I hired a CARPENTER to build me an armoire. He wouldn't let me have my freedom; he wanted to nail me down. But I saw through him. He was hammering away that I was screwing around. I finally became indignant and said: "Brother, you hit the nail on the head." That's when he left.

My apartment never really got finished, but I needed some electrical work done, so I called in an ELECTRICIAN. He had such charisma that the room would light up the moment he walked in. People were shocked when they heard I was dating him because he wasn't too bright. So I re-fused to make a commitment. All he wanted to do was plug it in, so I said, "Sock it to me, Baby!" Our affair was on and off, so I switched to someone else, and then I wired him that our relationship was over.

I next called in the WINDOW CLEANER. He said he was always looking out for me, but sometimes he was a real pane.

Maybe I was working ass backwards and should have started with painting and plastering the room first, but I did it later, figuring better late than never. When the PAINTER asked me out, I brushed him off. But the PAPER HANGER had me up against the wall when he was plastered.

I was getting nowhere trying to redecorate my entire apartment. It was too overwhelming, so I decided to concentrate my efforts on one room. My bedroom was the most neglected, so I started there. This is the room I use the most (need I say more). So, I started out by freshening up my bed.

My boyfriend the MATTRESS MAKER. Being with him was like eternal spring.

I needed a new blanket so I went shopping at a linen store. I met this BLANKET SALESMAN. Some guy, really! Whenever I caught him in a lie, he tried to cover up. The PILLOW MAKER always seemed depressed, he was a real downer. The chair in the room also looked shabby, so I telephoned a CHAIR DESIGNER. It didn't take long before I realized that he didn't have a leg to stand on, if he wanted to get serious. But when he said he wanted to date other women, it did not sit well with me.

One of my paintings looked faded and old, so I called in a FRAMER. He took to me immediately and said that I should have been in pictures.

The mirror in my bedroom was cracked; the building also looked after that. They sent in a MIRROR MAKER to replace the broken one. I couldn't trust him. I thought he was two-faced.

The summer was hot, and the room was stuffy, so I called in the AIR CONDITIONER INSTALLER. When our relationship got too hot, we decided to cool it.

I needed new keys for my door, as the building had changed them when they refurbished the halls. They supplied the LOCKSMITH. The key to our relationship was that he a-doored me, and he really latched on to me. My ceiling suddenly started leaking. I thought, *Dear God, not another repairman!* The PLUMBER was at my door in a jiffy, and I got to know him quite well. He was flush with his money and it all went down the drain. He had funny habits as well. He was always tapping me on the shoulder. What a drip! He did, however, shower me with gifts, and when he bought me a gift, it was toilet water.

While trying to correct the problems in my bathroom, I noticed that the soap dish was too small for my bars of soap. So I looked up SOAP MANUFACTURER in the yellow pages and called one to see if he could replace it with a larger one. He was always questioning me and told me to come clean. He really worked me up into a lather so I washed my hands clean of him.

My boyfriend the TOWEL MANUFACTURER. He had a dry sense of humor.

Because the plumber was unable to fix the leak in my bathroom, they sent in a ROOFER. Nice guy, but he wasn't in very good health. He came down with the shingles.

I thought of moving. Maybe this redecorating wasn't worth it. I noticed that a condo was being erected on the other side of town, nearer to my work, so I contacted the REAL ESTATE AGENT who liked me a lot. I went over one day, to see how things were progressing. I met the ARCHITECT. He happened to be on the premises at the time. We were introduced and he said he liked the way I was built. I fell for him like a ton of bricks. It didn't take long before he was making plans for our wedding. He was anxious to cement our relationship, but it just didn't stick. He was also having trouble with his erection.

I decided to stay in my apartment, and if I wasn't moving, I needed to have a car that was reliable. I considered buying a new one, so I went to the dealership. The CAR DEALER was always tooting his own horn. Although I really liked the car that I test drove, I decided to stick with what I had and take my car in for a maintenance check.

I tried to start it, but the battery was dead so I had it towed to the mechanic and then took a cab. The TAXI DRIVER was the worst. Whenever he went out on a date, he turned on the meter. I didn't think that was fare and he used to drive me crazy. When I arrived at my GARAGE MECHANIC, he checked the car and we began to talk. He said he was thinking of retiring, but I told him if he did, he'd be flat broke in no time. Those are the brakes! He was a funny guy. He had a great sense of humor, but when it came to telling jokes, I sure didn't take a back seat. By the way, I often wondered, *Do back seat drivers have longer arms*? No pun intended.

While hanging around the garage, my clothes got dirty and didn't smell too good, so I brought them to my DRY CLEANER. He said he could spot me a mile away. I didn't know if that was a compliment or some kind of dirty crack. I didn't press him on the issue, and we were able to iron things out.

Redecorating my bedroom and contemplating buying a new car certainly didn't take off, so I decided to work on my appearance. The more I was involved with men, the more I got to know them. Some of them were really cheap. They were only interested in one thing, if you get my drift. There was my boyfriend the PERFUME MANUFACTURER. He was so cheap, I couldn't get a scent out of him.

I thought I could change my look and maybe visit the WIG MAKER, but whenever we went out to dinner, he wanted me toupee. So, I went back to my HAIRDRESSER to get a new cut and style. He used to tease me a lot, and blow hot and cold. But I still liked him. I wanted our relationship to be permanent, but he cut it short. Sometimes I thought he really wasn't that nice. He would split hairs over everything, but at one time I thought I would dye for him. Finally, I gave him the brush off.

Next in my makeover was going through my cosmetics. Despite the fact that my COSMETICIAN and I fought a lot, he was always ready to make up.

For my next appointment, I went to my local BARBER. We were out one night, and we were almost involved in a serious accident. He said, "That was a close shave!" Then my nails needed some repairs, so I made an appointment with my MANICURIST, a male one, of course, so I told him off. I had the sense that if we married and he tried to nail me down, I would file for divorce. But there was something about him, I just couldn't put my finger on.

I was staying home a lot watching TV and was having trouble with my reception, so I called the TV REPAIRMAN. He became very remote when I tried to control him.

Having watched so much television, I became interested in sports so I started to go to all kinds of sports events. It didn't take long before I met a BASEBALL PLAYER. I really made a hit with him. He said I was on the ball. But then the team went on strike, so I didn't see much of him after that. I know that in baseball a player walks after four balls, but I sent him walking with two.

I became obsessed with sports games and I went to every sports event available. This obsession sure didn't hurt my social life. I went from one boyfriend to another. It was summertime, so outdoor sports were the thing. At a tennis match, I met the star TENNIS PLAYER, but I found out that he was in some kind of a racket, and I also told people that love meant nothing to him. I guess that was an advantage for him. But the net result made him a lonely man. The JOCKEY I met wasn't very nice. He was a racist. The GOLFER said he wasn't feeling very well. I thought, *Oh my God, I hope he doesn't have a stroke!* Nothing went right for him. He later told me he found a hole-in-one of his clubs. So much for him! The FOOTBALL PLAYER was really more fun to be with. I had heard that he played the field a lot but I gave him a run for his money. He was always trying to make a pass at me, but I really did get a big kick out of him. Then I met the CHAMPION SWIMMER. Whenever he took me out for the evening, we always ended up in a dive. And besides that, he was only interested in the breast stroke, mine. When we weren't eating in restaurants, we went to play pool.

As winter approached, sports games began to move indoors and this is where I met my boyfriend the HOCKEY PLAYER. He was a real cheap skate. One night we went to see one of his friends fight in a boxing match. I hadn't been to many, so watching it was really exciting. That night I broke up with the hockey player and started seeing the BOXER. He said I was a real knock out. So after dating him for several months, I told him it was time he bought me a ring. That was putting him up against the ropes.

My boyfriend the WRESTLER was a nervous wreck. I

told him to get a grip on himself. And the MARATHON RUNNER ran me ragged. I sure couldn't keep up with him. The winter was getting long, and I needed some exercise, so I decided to take to the ski hills where I met the SKIER. He gave me a lift for a while, but it was downhill after that. He never paid for my lift ticket, yet pretended to have money. It took me a while to catch on to his snow job.

I needed a vacation, so I decided to go to the country for a while. Before arriving at the farmhouse at which I was staying, I met the LUMBERJACK along the way. I didn't think our romance wood last. When he suggested a ménage-a-trois, I said I wasn't interested in a tree-o.

I rented a lovely room at a motel and decided to take a walk one day. Who did I come across? This handsome FARMER. So we started dating. I didn't ask, but I had the feeling he was married, because he seemed hen pecked. He was getting very serious with me, so I told him not to count his chickens before they hatch. I wasn't very nice. I milked him for all he was worth. But he said it was only a drop in the bucket. He came across as somewhat of a cow-ard. I decided to leave him, but due to all the walking on the farm, I developed a corn and decided to look after my feet.

So I made an appointment with a PODIATRIST. He didn't have a nice personality. He seemed kind of callous, and he had a corny sense of humor. After dating him a while, he wanted me to toe the line, so I put my foot down and walked away. However, he said that there was some medication that might help my feet, so I went to my PHARMACIST. We started going out together, but he was really weird. He wanted to have sex three times a day before meals. He was a real pill! I just couldn't swallow it any longer, so I left him and gave him a taste of his own medicine.

After a string of bad affairs, I know that I promised myself I would stay away from doctors but I still ached for them. I had my annual appointment with my OBSTETRICIAN/GYNECOLOGIST who wasn't very funny at telling jokes, but his delivery was good. But he couldn't put my finger on what I didn't like about him. I realized that I found fault with a lot of my boyfriends' characteristics and qualities.

The PLASTIC SURGEON was always handing me a line. I said to him, "Just take a look at my face, because brother, when it comes to lines, there's no contest!" The UROLOGIST was very complimentary, he said I was the specimen of womanhood. He had funny eating habits though. When we went out for dinner he always ordered pee soup as the entrée and pee-can pie for dessert. Although not a medical man I liked my CHIROPODIST, but nothing came from that relationship, as we started off on the wrong foot. My boyfriend the DIETICIAN was starving for my affection. He was eating himself up, but before we broke up he did suggest that I eat more fruit. My obsession with doctors was becoming problematic so I visited my PSYCHIATRIST. He told me I was a narcissist. I didn't like this diagnosis and I gave him a piece of my mind and decided that I preferred the dietician's advice and went to buy some high-fiber, low-fat foods.

The ORANGE JUICE MAKER became my latest squeeze. I had a real crush on him. At the outdoor market

I met the FRUIT VENDOR. He was very cute. He asked if he could kiss me and I said, "Please honeydew!" He was pressuring me to marry him and I said, "I cantelope." So I stopped dating him. Too bad, we would have made a cute pear. At times, I couldn't fig-ure him out as he was always raisin' hell.

Although I was still eating a lot of fruit, I was told to eat a lot of fish. So, I met this FISHMONGER. He was very fin-nicky, he said I smelt, which wasn't very nice of him! But, he also confessed he loved me body and sole. He would always flounder when I asked him for a commitment. He was quite a piker when it came to spending money. However, I did meet some FISHERMEN. One was always handing me a line, but the other wormed his way into my heart. I was easy bait.

Because I had a lot of fruit in my house, I began to notice little insects crawling around. I called in my EXTERMINATOR to see what the problem was. He wasn't very nice. Whenever I told him about the ants, he told me to bug off. That didn't help, so through mail order, I bought some money back guaranteed solution to kill ants. I waited daily for the POSTMAN. He was the strangest mail I ever met. He had to put his stamp of approval on everything I did. He thought he was letter perfect, however, he said that if I ever became pregnant, he would send me away so that I could have a special delivery.

The diet was one thing, but I needed exercise as well, so I started going to the gym. The AEROBICS INSTRUCTOR was taken with me right away. He said he would bend over backwards for me, but I thought that was stretching a point, and besides, he was always jumping to conclusions.

I also started riding my bicycle more often, but my boyfriend the BICYCLE MAKER was a real wheeler-dealer. Would you believe, I even went in for Karate? I started dating the KARATE TEACHER, but I left him after a while. I didn't get a kick out of him anymore. I thought massages would be good for me, but when I started dating the MASSEUSE he really rubbed me the wrong way. So much for my physical fitness program.

I got tired of the healthy stuff and was dying for some good meat and bread and pastry. That's what I really liked and maybe that would improve my mood. I went to my local BUTCHER and inquired about the best cuts of meat. He was a young, shy kind of guy. He couldn't re-veal his true feelings for me, but it was obvious that he cared. Then I realized he was a chronic complainer, he was always beefing about something. He really had a problem with his shyness, so I suggested he try acting. This way he could ham it up. But when it came to auditioning, he chickened out. I decided to break up with him cold turkey.

Although I was watching my diet very carefully, I was dying for a hot dog. I met this HOT DOG VENDOR, we were on a roll for a while, but I didn't relish anything permanent. But the FRENCH FRY MAKER ate so quickly I couldn't ketchup to him.

Next, I was off to the bakery. When I first met the BAKER, he tried very hard to impress me. He said he was rolling in dough, but I told him I didn't knead any. He also tried to butter me up by telling me I was his roll model. But in all fairness, he was well bread. It didn't take long before I got bored with his knead to impress me, so I went next door to his friend the CANDY MAKER. When I told him I was sweet on him, he believed me. What a sucker!

The PASTRY CHEF drank a lot. He was pie-eyed half the time, but his baking took the cake. I love coffee and my boyfriend the COFFEE BEAN GROWER sure knew how to urn a living.

Once I was back to eating what I really liked, I started cooking again and was looking for new recipes. I saw a cute CHEF on television, so I made a point to meet him. I was surprised when I first saw him. He wasn't very tall, so they made him a short-order cook. It didn't take long before I got fed up with him. He was always in a stew about something. Whenever he made a stir fry, he told me to take a wok. But I did find out that he was a chef at a bed-and-breakfast place, so I checked in for a night. The next morning, it was pretty cold out, so I thought a nice, hot bowl of oatmeal would be good. When I tasted it, it was so bad, I couldn't eat it. I was beginning to think he was also a cereal killer. I checked out early and said, "Cheerio!"

That kind of turned me off to eating in and trying new recipes. So I decided to eat out one night, and went to the restaurant in a well known hotel. I met this cute WAITER. I had heard that he played the horses, so I was surprised when he asked me for a tip. The HOTEL OWNER was suite, but I didn't have room for him in my life.

After pigging out on food, I decided to do something cultural, so I attended some concerts to learn to appreciate music. That started a whole new list of boyfriends.

There was the PIANO PLAYER. Even though I was instrumental in getting his career started, he was a very messy guy. He could never remember where he left his stool, and he was also forgetful, he could never find his keys. When we had sex, he would ask me if it was upright. I said, "Baby, it's grand!" The VIOLINIST was so sweet. He said he would never string me along and also made it very clear to me that there were no strings attached. No need to tell you what the DRUMMER said to me, "Beat it!" My boyfriend the HARPIST was a terrible lyre. And the SAXOPHONE PLAYER was always tooting his own horn.

While I was at the concerts and into that milieu, I met the ORCHESTRA LEADER. He was strange. When he hurt my feelings, he gave me a Band-aid. His SINGER wasn't much better. When we had an argument, he became very vocal. The SONG WRITER and I started off on the wrong note, but then we made beautiful music together, and the D.J. and I used to go around a lot. After one performance at the ballet, I met the BALLET DANCER. He was always on his toes and he was tu-tu cute!

While in this cultural bit, I met an English ACTOR. Every time we had a fight, it was quite a scene. I thought he was quite ordinary, but he thought he was a Great Britain. And the MOVIE CRITIC, I couldn't picture myself with him, because the whole affair seemed like quite an act. The THEATER USHER always wanted to walk me down the aisle. But he wasn't so nice to me. Whenever I stood up, he told me to be seated.

I decided to attend the opening of an exhibition. The

ARTIST was present to speak to the public and I made a point of approaching him. He was a real heartthrob, much older than I, but there was still life in him. He was sensitive like most artists and I knew that I would easel-y upset him if I brushed him off. The CALENDAR PRINTER was some sort of artist himself. When I told him I missed my monthly period, it took years off his life and it left him week. He walked around as if in a days.

Today photography is considered an art. The PHOTOGRAPHER had such a negative attitude, but I still liked him, although nothing ever developed from our relationship. I couldn't picture myself with him on any permanent basis, but I took a shot at it. The TATTOO ARTIST needled me a lot. And he sure left his mark on me.

The circus came to town once a year and I knew the CIRCUS OWNER very well. We dated every time he came to our city. He kept me on a tight rope, but I fell for him anyway. He used to clown around a lot, but that was O.K. with me too. One of the circus acts involved a VENTRILOQUIST. He was always putting words in my mouth. He must have thought I was some kind of a dummy. This circus also had a FORTUNE TELLER as an added attraction. He had me in the palm of his hand, but there was no future with him. Another act in the circus was a magic act. The MAGICIAN and I dated a lot, but when he pulled this gorgeous girl out of a hat, I thought it was time for me to disappear. There was also a HYPNOTIST. He got angry when I wouldn't go to sleep with him.

I was so busy dating and going to events, that I neglected some of my clothes and wardrobe. My bras looked worn, my shoes and slippers looked shabby and my dresses looked out of date. So I got busy shopping and as a result met many more different men. To start, there was the BRASSIERE MAKER. I liked him because he gave me a lift, but we busted up after a few months. We really didn't make a very good pair. I had a run in with the HOSIERY MANUFACTURER and after that he kept stocking me. With the SHOEMAKER, I had better luck. He was head over heels in love with me and said I was his sole mate. Straight laced, my foot! I found out he was a bootlegger! However, the SLIPPER MAKER was not so easy to get along with. He was as stubborn as a mule.

Not having such good fortune with my undergarments and footwear, I thought I would now take a stab at my wardrobe as my sweaters were looking a little out dated. The SWEATER MANUFACTURER was a real knit picker. He thought I was reckless when I drove and would always tell me to pull over. What a knit wit! The DRESS DESIGNER I dated said he didn't like the clothes I was wearing. He said they weren't in vogue anymore. Although he would hem and haw about our relationship, I remained true to him in my fashion. I was luckier with my TAILOR. He was a very funny guy. He kept me in stitches, but our sex life was sew-sew. I used to needle him a lot about that, but based on our relationship he didn't seam to mind. After dating for quite a while, we realized we weren't suited for one another. My MILLINER was on top of it all. When I needed him, he came running at the drop of a hat. He was always headed in the right direction. The PURSE MANUFACTURER was optimistic.

He thought our relationship was in the bag. My wardrobe was picking up nicely.

Now I had to accessorize, so I met with the JEWELER, who specialized in pearls. He tried to string me along, but I was too cultured for that. I heard that he was into something illegal and that he was the ring leader. But he was no dummy; he was always on the watch. Our friendship became jaded, but in all fairness, he was an o' pal of mine. When you got down to the nitty gritty, he was a diamond in the rough. When I told him I liked silver jewelry, he recommended a SILVERSMITH. He immediately took a shine to me. He said I had sterling qualities, but he had no polish. He would run around yelling, "Hi Ho Silvo!" Oh, and my FURRIER. He was an eager beaver and quite foxy at times. At other times, he was like a little lamb, but he did have a broadtail, if you pardon the expression. I really had to hand it to the GLOVE MANUFACTURER. He had a finger on everything.

After spending all that money on my new look, I needed an ACCOUNTANT to check my financial situation. He was very suspicious of my behavior. He said something didn't add up. So I said, "I don't like the way you look at other figures." That was a total disaster.

I needed some solace and peace of mind in my life. I thought seeing a RABBI was a good start. After preaching to me for a while, we started seeing each other socially. We dated twice a week, religiously, but then I got tired of him trying to reform me. He started to complain about having headaches. I asked him if it was in his temple. Then he wanted to know if I was seeing anyone besides hymn. I swore on the Bible that I wasn't. I also told him that I worshipped the ground that he walked on. For some reason he didn't believe in me and we parted as friends.

I reached the point where I had to do some thinking and to find other more internal ways to occupy my mind. Bridge seemed to be the answer, as a lot of my friends were taking lessons. I found a wonderful BRIDGE TEACHER. I knew he played around a lot and naturally he made a pass at me and I knew he had a few tricks up his sleeves. After the lesson I went to the library so that I could brush up on some of the rules. The LIBRARIAN started to date me and would book me days in advance. The book I took out from the library was falling apart, so I went and bought some glue. The GLUE MANUFACTURER became very attached to me but he didn't stick around very long.

Mental gymnastics obviously wasn't the answer, and I was beginning to think that a dog might give me comfort. They say a dog is man's best friend, and I hoped even a woman's. I needed some diversion and besides I had previously been a pet owner and I really liked animals. I went to the local pet shop and there in a cage was the sweetest, most affectionate loving puppy. I knew I had to have him. I had to visit the VETERINARIAN to update my puppy on all his shots. After a few visits I got to know the vet, but all he wanted to do was pet. I told him he was barking up the wrong tree and besides I thought he was quite catty, although he thought he was purr-fect. Whenever it poured, he said it was raining cats and dogs. I stopped dating him when I found out he was horsing around. I got that information from his parrot. My DOG

TRAINER wasn't much better. When I asked him to loan me some money, there was a long paws.

Every day new changes occurred in my life. One of my friend's brothers was arrested during some kind of riot. So, I went with her to bail him out. The first thing I saw was the handsome PRISON GUARD. People thought that it was a crime that I was dating him, but he would call me everyday from his cell phone. Some people were not very nice. They would tease me and ask, "Is your boyfriend still in jail?" He was also moody at times and when something upset him, he would lock himself in his room for days.

While waiting for him to get off duty one day, one of the inmates, an ARSONIST, was being released after having served his time in prison. I began dating him, but that affair went up in flames. It was actually too bad that we broke it off, because people thought we would make a very good match. I did start dating his cell mate the THIEF, but he said that I was too old for him. He liked to rob the cradle.

From one extreme to the other, prison guard to arsonist to gambling—that was my life! I decided to try my luck at the casino. After dating the CASINO OWNER for a while, I realized that he was full of crap and I told him so. The CASHIER at the casino wasn't much better. He was a real looney and didn't have many cents. Frequenting this establishment, naturally I met up with a GAMBLER. He was a very devoted nephew. He was always talking about his auntie. He took a chance on our relationship but the odds were against him. I began betting at the roulette table. The CROUPIER and I hit it off immediately, but when we went out for dinner, he wanted me to chip in.

I was beginning to lose self respect and feel like a loser. I was susceptible and I got involved with a real rough crowd, although it seemed exciting at the time. I met this COCAINE DEALER and when he asked me to go steady with him I said I would take a crack at it. Then he introduced me to a GUN MANUFACTURER who was always loaded and would always shoot his mouth off. That wasn't bad enough. He introduced me to a TERRORIST. Dating him was a blast but he exploded when I told him I wouldn't see him anymore. The BOOTLEGGER would wine and dine me at times, but he was pretty Scotch when it came to big spending.

The POLICE eventually caught on to their scam and busted the whole lot of them. As I was associated with this group, I was a star witness and had to be interrogated by the police. The first CONSTABLE I met asked me out after the arraignment. When I asked him for a commitment, he said he wasn't ready. What a cop out! He seemed really tired. I think he needed arrest. The DETECTIVE on the case was an easier mark, but when it came to love making, he didn't have a clue. On my way home from the station, I was pulled over for speeding. The TRAFFIC COP who stopped me was different. He tried to speed up our relationship but I told him to stop.

I was advised to leave town for a while until things cooled down with gang drug dealing. I packed my bags and took a bus to the train station. The BUS DRIVER was kind of fresh. I thought he went too far. He didn't know when to stop, so I told him where to get off. When we arrived at the station, the PORTER took my luggage. He had a grip on me immediately. He was obviously well trained. His two mistakes were that he thought our relationship was in the bag and it was hard to keep track of him. The train took me to the airport to begin my holiday in the islands.

When I arrived there, they told me that my plane was delayed due to adverse weather conditions. The air traffic controller put me in touch with a METEOROLOGIST who I happened to know through a friend. He used to shower me with gifts, but that soon cooled off. He was moody, he used to blow hot and cold. Besides, when I was in a good mood, he would always rain on my parade, not to mention, he was long winded.

My boyfriend the WEATHERMAN. Getting him to fall for me was a breeze. But our relationship became quite stormy.

I waited for the boarding call for my plane and when it was to board, I met the PILOT. He said he had a stop-over at my destination and asked if I would be interested in spending some time with him during my vacation. We met for dinner and boy, was he moody! He was always up in the air about something. I told him to relax and come down to earth. Dating him wasn't much fun. He didn't have much energy. We would order in supper early, and he wanted to know the ETA. Then he would crash out at 7:00. And whenever we made love, he'd yell, "I'm coming in for a landing!" He was really a very plane guy.

There was a space camp near the resort at which I was staying, and I went to visit. There I met the ASTRONAUT. I thought he was out of this world, and when we dined out, the sky was the limit. He loved buying me chocolates, especially Mars bars and Milky Ways. Then there was a short affair with a SEISMOLOGIST. He said he would move heaven and earth for me.

When I got back from my trip, I decided to check up on my health again, as I was feeling a tad out of sorts. Maybe it was jet lag, or I picked up a bug in the islands, but I wanted to be sure. My hearing wasn't great so I naturally attributed it to the flight. Just in case, I thought I should see an AUDIOLOGIST. He was very complimentary. He knew what I wanted to hear. I would always say, "That sounds good to me." When he wasn't nice to me, I would get angry and turn a deaf ear. He noticed something in my eye and sent me to an OPHTHALMOLOGIST. He was so critical. He said he didn't like the way I looked. I accepted that because I thought he was so handsome, I just couldn't take my eyes off of him. But I knew he was for me in the blink of an eye. When I went to get my new glasses, the OPTICIAN and I didn't see eye to eye on anything. No need to pursue that affair—check ups, check ups, no end to it!

My knees began to hurt, I thought it was because of all the walking I had done in the Bahamas. The ORTHOPEDIC SURGEON was very funny. I did a little acting. So, whenever I was about to go on stage, he would tell me to "break a leg". Then on to the EAR, NOSE, AND THROAT SPECIALIST. When I heard he was cheating on me, I found that pretty hard to swallow. I found him nosey and very vocal. But he said he saw some inflammation so he sent me to the RADIOLOGIST. I couldn't fool him, he said he could see right through me.

I hadn't had much experience with military men, so I started to look around. I went down to the local army base and met a cute SOLDIER. We clicked right away and he asked me to join the army. I said I would take a whack at it. The SAILOR was my next conquest. Every time they shipped him out, I would wave good-bye and say, "I'll sea you soon."

Don't for one minute think all my relationships were frivolous. My boyfriend the MASON, he was stoned half the time, but our relationship was monumental. I knew his father and he was a chip off the old block. Things were different with the MINER. He accused me of being a gold digger, just because I asked him to buy me a bunch of carats. The MATADOR that I dated was another story. If I looked at another guy, he would see red and that's no bull.

Neglect, neglect, my middle name. My garden looked awfully seedy—you should pardon the pun. I wanted to plant some new trees on my property. My boyfriend the FORESTER was always trying to impress me with his family tree. However, he was a hard worker, and when he went to bed, he slept like a log. He also said that if I ever left him, he would pine away for me.

Then I called my GARDENER to take a look at my garden. I really didn't like him very much. He was always trying to dig up some dirt about me. I thought my FLORIST would be more of a help. Things were rose-y with us for a while, but then I realized he was only interested in my two-lips.

When I got back from the florist, my telephone wasn't working, so I called my TELEPHONE OPERATOR. He had a lot of hang ups, and he was always handing me a line and always giving me options. When he said he wouldn't marry me, I let him off the hook. Just as soon as my phone was working, I got a call from one of my friends. Don't be shocked, but a girlfriend, whose father had just died. Naturally I went to the funeral and there I met the UNDERTAKER. He wasn't too well, he was always coffin. There was something else about him that was odd, he didn't open up much and it made me think that he had a skeleton in his closet. When I told him a joke, he had a deadpan face. When our situation became grave, he told me to drop dead. I briefly dated the guy who was running the CREMATORIUM, but he was so rigid, that he thought every day was Ash Wednesday.

When my boyfriend the COMEDIAN was at the local club, he asked me to come out and see the show. His performance in bed was just for laughs. He didn't realize that the joke was on him when I walked in with my date, the RADIO ANNOUNCER—a very sexy guy. He was funnier than the comedian. When I asked him why he had such small hands, he said, "Brief paws for station identification!"

I should really tell you about some of my short relationships. No, I'm not going to say I went out with a MIDGET and that he accused me of always looking down on him. No, I'm not going to mention that this was a short affair. But there was the POPCORN MAKER that I dated. They promoted him to a kernel. The COMPUTER EXPERT was as quiet as a mouse. The DELI MAN didn't like cigarettes, but he did admit that he smoked meat. And the LAMP MAKER, his reputation was a little shady. I liked the ELEVATOR OPERATOR. We had our ups and downs, so I finally told him where to get off. My boyfriend the ANTIQUE DEALER said he preferred older women. The CROSSWORD PUZZLE CREATOR was feeling very down, when I wouldn't come across, but he was no square.

The WRITER was stubborn. He would never admit he was wrong. Originally we started out as pen pals and the rest is quite a story. The PUBLISHER was always paging me. I could never trust him, he was always telling tall tales. He was really one for the books.

The COWBOY liked to horse around a lot, but he wasn't going to rope me in. The FULLER BRUSH man. He wasn't so unusual, just knock on any door. He told me that he also sold brooms and that he was very lucky. He won a sweepstake. And then there was the ZOOKEEPER. I couldn't bear being with him, because he was always lion to me. Other times, he was really a deer. While at the zoo, I met the BEE KEEPER, but I was allergic to him, I kept breaking out in hives. The SHEPHERD was a little lamb, but I couldn't pull the wool over his eyes.

After a session with the MEMBER OF PARLIAMENT, I couldn't wait for our next session. The DONKEY DRIVER was a real pain in the ass. And the LADDER MAKER was rushing me. I told him to take it one step at a time. The SKY DIVER wasn't a bad sort. He was really very down to earth. I couldn't get a straight word out of the STUTTERER. Every time the NATIVE AMERICAN and I went to dinner, he would make a reservation. And the GARBAGE COLLECTOR. He dumped me after a few dates and said I was nothing but trash. I didn't give up so fast. I asked if I could be recycled.

Wow! I'm exhausted and I don't think I want to date for quite some time! I'll take a good rest for about three or four days.